The Broken Buddha

The Broken Buddha

Poems

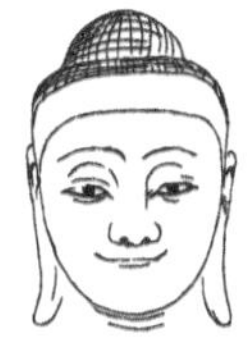

Johnny Cordova

Roadside Press

Cover Art: Harim Choi, gouache and pencil on paper.
Cover & Interior Design: Dominique Ahkong
Author Photo: Dominique Ahkong
Editor: Michele McDannold

Roadside Press
Meredosia, Illinois
roadsidefam.com

In memory of Amber Piccola

This dewdrop world—
Is a dewdrop world,
And yet, and yet . . .

— KOBAYASHI ISSA

Contents

III. ASHES

The Broken Buddha

I bought him because after two centuries
of sitting in silent stone meditation
in a remote mountain temple
in a remote province of Burma
he was moved for cleaning by a careless
monk who let his mind wander
and went tumbling down a staircase
with the Buddha in his arms.

I bought him because after presiding over
generations of prostrate monks
breathing them in and breathing out
he sat in the public bazaar year after year
head glued back in place
waiting to be claimed.

I bought him because the art collectors
could not see the passage of so many lives
carved into the white marble of his eyes.
They took one look at the crooked
cracked line around his neck
and did not want him.

I bought him because I too missed a step
and went crashing down some stairs
my love in my arms
and could not be put back
together.

I bought him because I failed to stand
strong in the heart when it mattered
and let my mind wander into
a dreamland.

I bought him because when I awoke there
I'd gone too far to get back.
The dream had become my new world
and I wander there now ruined
through the wreckage of my burning.

I bought him because once one is broken
one stays broken
even when they are able to glue
your head back on.

I bought him because for a long time
he has been sitting in brokenness
without needing to be claimed
without needing wholeness.

I bought him because I want him to teach me.

I bought him because he was broken.

Author's Note

Though the poems in the first section of this book are set in Thailand and greater Southeast Asia, they take inspiration from classic Zen stories of Japanese monks who scaled monastery walls to drink rice wine and cavort all night with prostitutes in comfort houses. They are best read as 21st-century renderings of an age-old striving to reconcile commitment to a spiritual path with what Zen calls "the red thread of passion."

I. All Night Rain

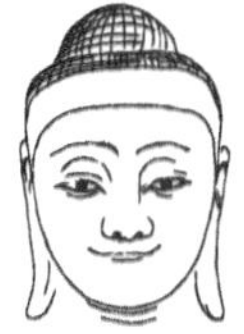

Nana

You've just returned to Bangkok
on the overnight train
from ten days of meditation
in a forest monastery where you sat
with Thai monks, hour upon hour,
right knee throbbing from old injury
until the pain became mere sensation.

You check into a room in Nana
before making your way through
a back-alley soi, past the blowjob bars,
to the go-go bars at Nana Plaza
and take a seat in a neon-lit cave
where very young women from upcountry
stand on long narrow stages
shoulder to shoulder between polished chrome poles
topless in skintight bottoms
with long black hair and wandering eyes,
hips swaying off-rhythm to American pop music
like row boats tied to a dock on a shoreline.

And though you've been here before
you see in a moment of perfect clarity
that it is not a doorway
to the mysteries of woman—what Camille Paglia
promised—as much as a second-class ticket
to a realm of hungry ghosts
where endless desperate searching
is never satisfied.

And as you down another beer
you understand why Deshimaru
had his Zen students meet him
in the strip clubs of Paris
and told them it was the perfect place to practice.

You also understand that despite your
insight you will pay someone's bar fine,
perhaps the one who is older than the others,
clear-eyed and stage-savvy, fluid,
with muscled calves and dark brown nipples,
whose hand on your thigh as she orders a "lady drink"
gives you more than mere sensation.

You know as you contemplate
the emptiness of all phenomena
that you will take her back to your room
and watch from the bed
as she emerges from the bathroom
freshly showered, nudity concealed
by an oversized bath towel, inexplicably shy
despite having enacted this intimacy
with hundreds of men
hundreds of times prior.

You will ask for 69
because you've learned
that it is better that way in these situations.
She will lower her ass onto your face,
as you part those fine hairs with your tongue
and it will slowly dawn on you
that she tastes like Tom Yum Goong,
what she must have had for dinner,

and you will marvel at the improbability
of ever loving Thai food
as much as you do at that moment.

After an hour or so of mutual pleasure,
her juices all over your chin,
she will rise from the bed and say,
You very good!
as she bounds off to the bathroom
for another shower.
She will stand by the door in street clothes,
small black purse dangling
by a chain from her shoulder,
as you place 2,000 Baht in her hand,
her asking price for short time.
She will place the prize in her purse
and smile with impeccable grace
and put her hands together to wai you
as she says, *Thank you for you,*
then disappears down the hallway.

In the morning you will stuff
a notebook and toothbrush into a backpack
with your unlaundered meditation clothes
and catch the BTS train to the airport
where you will board a flight to Singapore,
back to your job teaching hot yoga
to women in designer bikinis
who will ask how your retreat went.

After stowing your bag in an overhead bin
you will look out upon takeoff
from your window seat

at the sprawling Bangkok metropolis,
noting how the roads turn to dirt
on the outskirts of the city,
how houses become huts,
freshwater canals snaking their way between them,
each hut adorned with a red clay roof,
the landscape beyond dotted with temples
and stand-alone trees, impossibly flat,
stretching farther than the eyes can follow,
centuries back through time
before Buddhism arrived by sea
to a world awash with longing.

Foot Massage

Some things are constant.
The oppressiveness of heat,
the darkening of light,
the low humming roar of late-afternoon traffic
in Bangkok.
You hear it through the glass,
like waves pressing into your mind,
as you drift in and out of consciousness.
A girl with thick eyebrows and very gentle hands
caresses your calf muscle,
slides down around the heel of your foot
in long, firm strokes.
Each time you open your eyes, she smiles.
Her beauty is giving in a world that takes.
It begins to rain, suddenly,
a hammering, blanket rain,
the sound of it drowning all other sounds beneath it.
Someone opens the door and it crashes in.
The door closes and the room again becomes a womb.

Nana Entertainment Plaza

Feral cats, scrawny, wild-eyed
on rooftop ledges, down narrow sois,
hunting the rat. Isaan girls with jet-black
hair, from northern jungles,
on sidewalks, in go-go bars, sitting
outside massage parlors.
Hello welcome!
You handsome man!
I go with you!
The loneliest White man in the world,
Naughty Boy's Guide in hand,
drunk-stained, sweating Viagra,
searching for mercy between young girls' thighs.
The Buddha in every temple, on every corner,
in every Thai whore's heart, stone-faced,
looking down through centuries, unshaken,
because this matter of survival, this wretched
stinking play, is nobody's fate
but a tide rolling in to roll back out again.

Li Po took the overnight train

from Bangkok to Chiang Mai. And wrote poems along the way. He'd write one in his notebook, rip out the page, toss it out the window, watch the wind sweep it away. Then he'd write another, making offering after offering to the green on green of rice fields, to the sloping, dancing rooftops of temples, to great golden Buddhas that shone and glistened in the Theravāda sun. When the day darkened, an attendant came and converted his seat to a bunk bed. Li Po sat cross-legged behind the curtain, meditating on the days of the Tang dynasty, then lay down to dream. The jostling of the rails became the stops and starts of his sleep.

All Night Rain

All night rain in the jungle.
Relentless, pressing the earth,
not taking no for an answer.
The windows of this hut are open-air,
mosquito screens the only shield between
the heat, the sound, the smell of rain.
Rain bursting forth from black sky,
bending giant ferns. Rain through
giant sprawling trees,
pouring off the roof in sheets.
All night, rain in my dreams.
Each time I awake rain
without cease.
The longer it rains, this endless giving,
this thundering concert of creation,
the more it resembles revelation.
Like a rice farm girl
you meet in a bar
who comes to your bed
and does not leave
for days. The smell of her neck
all over the sheets. This rain
coming down, emphatic,
all-knowing, the constant
hammering pattering
drumming of it.
In the morning I feel drunk
from rain. Even now,
sitting zazen, it comes.
Rain rising up my spine.
She has entered here
like rain.

Thai Monks

I meet with a group of Thai monks,
mostly young men in their 20s
and teenage boys
who want to practice their English.
We gather in a loose circle
under a sprawling tree
in a corner of their monastery.

First, the usual questions:
What is your favorite Thai food?
Why do you live in Thailand?
Why do you shave your head?
Do you want to be a monk?

Then the conversation turns to giggles:
Do you have a girlfriend?
Will you marry a Thai woman?
What is sex like?

That last one.
I don't have the heart to tell them,
so I phrase my answer as best I can
in dharmic terms:
When you can't have it
sex is the biggest thing in your mind, I say.
When you can have it any time
it's just like anything else,
an ordinary part of life.

They grow quiet, contemplating
my attempt at wisdom.

Then the next question:
Are Thai women good at sex?

Everyone erupts in laughter.

Ryokan owns a barbershop

tucked into a narrow soi in Saphan Khwai, where I live. I visit him once a week and ask him to shave my head with a straight razor. I love the way he meditates on the grain, the steady touch of his fingers, the way the blade feels sliding over my skin.

There is an antique barber's chair and a sink, a small wooden bench against the wall, a bamboo mat on the floor where Ryokan sits and takes his lunch. The sign over the door says *Great Barber*. When he is finished shaving my head, he trims my eyebrows and massages coconut oil into my scalp. "Now you can be a monk," he whispers in my ear. He makes the same joke every week. Giggling as if it were the first time he's thought about it.

Old Abbot

You know it's the old abbot
by the sound of his footsteps
as he approaches from the rear
along the side of the open-air
meditation hall.
He barely lifts his feet when he walks,
his sandals sliding along the sand,
his gait even, unwavering.
When he reaches the front
you open your eyes and watch
as he lifts the bottom of his robe,
slowly climbs onto the wooden dais,
crosses his legs into full lotus position.
Behind him is a grove of trees.
Beyond the trees a pond.
Beyond the pond a jungle.
He begins to speak in simple English,
his accent so thick, pronunciation so Thai,
you are lucky to follow a third
of what he is saying.
You don't mind this at all.
You like to look at him.
There is a lifetime of radical commitment
tangible in his body.

Full Moon Morning

The morning after the moon
filled the sky
with blue light,
the pond is perfectly still,
as if satiated.

A small turtle stretches its neck
out of the water,
looks around,
goes back under.

You return from walking meditation
to the open-air hall
for sitting meditation,
find your place in the sand
and settle in.

The old abbot has been on the dais
since you left, in full lotus,
for more than an hour,
shoulders slumped,
head bobbing up and down.

Oh, Abbot, what were you up to
with the moon last night?

Ode to a British Monk

How easy to renounce this world. To drop a blue passport into a government bin and pull the dust-orange robe of a mendicant monk over your shoulder. To make your bed in a bamboo hut in a forest and face the night alone. To face oneself by oneself. To let the sorrows of the world creep in and pass through you like tropical rain. To walk five miles each morning, begging bowl in hand, eating one meal a day, before noon. As Thai girls travel by train from village to city, offering the dark red fruit of their bodies to the hands of hungry men. Did you attend that feast of fingertip pleasures and finally have your fill? Did you find it lacking from the beginning? How did you decide, as a very young man, that emptiness feels fuller in the hand than having, or even wanting? Afternoons you appear at Suan Mokkh International Dhamma Hermitage and talk in front of backpackers, tourists, and seekers on their first meditation retreats. You do it as a favor to the old abbot, with whom you shared a teacher some twenty years before. You give sublime elucidations on the practice of Anapanasati—mindfulness with breathing—but mostly you point out the pitfalls of the path, making jokes about people performing walking meditation as if they are holding uncracked eggs between their arse cheeks. You do this every day for nine days, and on the tenth day, when the retreatants have broken silence, many will call you arrogant, cynical, condescending. "I hated him!" a young American woman will say. By that time you will be back in your hut in the forest, sitting on a worn cushion, right foot over left in the eternal posture, sitting as if the sitting is forever, completely unconcerned with the things people think about you.

The young monk rings the bell

rings the bell
rings the bell
rings the bell.

The old monk rings the bell
one time

and everybody hears it.

Ikkyu walked into a ladyboy bar

on the dark side of Bangkok and ordered a double shot of Johnnie Walker Black. He drank it neat, no chaser, then walked to the end of the bar and rang a shiny brass bell that hung by a rope from the ceiling. It meant a free round of drinks for everyone, on Ikkyu's tab. All the ladyboys cheered.

A group of ladyboys in high-heeled shoes and skintight finery crowded around Ikkyu's barstool, fresh drinks in hand, and fawned over him. One rubbed his shoulders. One massaged his thigh. Another whispered in his ear, with her limited English, all the nasty things she wanted to do with him. So many bewitching ladyboys offering their marvelous bodies for his pleasure. He could not choose just one. Then the tallest one, with high cheekbones and a take-charge smile, lifted her skirt and placed her long brown cock in Ikkyu's hand. It was hot and girthy and stiffened in his palm like a prayer. Ikkyu looked into her eyes. She looked deep into his. The night was a pirate's map of hidden treasures.

Ode to a Bangkok Ladyboy

Tourists, mostly men, line up to pose with you for photos they'll send home for a laugh with the boys. Women too, who envy your easy glamour, your confidence, the way you flaunt your assets shamelessly, with humor. You make a living along the Sukhumvit corridor, in late-night bars, from curious straight men who find you on dating apps. You can be bottom. You can be top. You are a wish-fulfilling genie free of the lamp that contained you. Mornings you sleep past noon before bringing flowers to your neighborhood temple, where you pray to the Buddha, and his guardians, to protect your spirit. You take rice, then walk your sister's children home from school, tend to them into the evening. You disappear for weeks at a time to a monastery upcountry that lets you sit on the women's side during meditation. You make it easy for me to love you.

In a Silent Way

After lovemaking, she dresses.
Hit and run, she says, grinning
as you walk her down to the road
to catch a taxi.
Her parents don't know she's seeing a man.
They think she goes out with friends
after Poetry Club.
"Poetry Club" has been meeting
multiple times a week.

Back in your rented room
above the Kallang River
black strands of hair adorn the floor.
You think of her body face down
on your bed, the tilt of her hips,
the fine lines of Asian pubic hair.
You think of how you sat together
without talking, savoring
the red earth layers of natural wine,
contemplating jazz.
You think of the ways she moaned
when you touched her.

You decide against turning off
the red lamp on your bedside table.
You leave Miles Davis on repeat,
at a barely perceptible volume.
You want the mood to linger.

Later, you are awakened by thunder,

a sudden bursting tropical rain.
You open your eyes and see
the room aglow in red, the curved neck
of the bottle on your desk.
You touch your fingers to your face
and smell her, close your eyes
and listen to the rain
beating down on everything.

Then it stops, the rain,
as suddenly as it began,
and the room again is silent.
The soft rolling trill of keyboards,
muted notes of a trumpet
rise up to your ears,
penetrate your dreams
for the rest of the night
as you drift in and out of sleep.

Yangon

The first thing you do
when you've checked into your guest house
is fuck
on the king-size mattress
that lies close to the floor
beneath an antique ceiling fan,
her head hanging over the edge,
black hair pooled in long swirls
on the white tiles.
You reach for the sloping rise of her breasts,
her nipples stiff and wanting,
as you savor the cream of her cunt.
When you enter her she moans.
You try to make it last
as she wraps her legs around you.

In the night you wander
the labyrinth streets of Yangon
in search of something to eat.
You find a dimly-lit stall on a corner
near a hilltop where a young Burmese mother
serves Mohinga, a thick tangy soup,
in big steaming bowls with noodles
and an egg in it.
It's better than any she's had, she says.
You are pleased to see her happy.

For dessert you buy durian
in a back-alley soi
from a shirtless boy with a machete.

He stands beneath a bare bulb
clipped onto the side of a building
as he splits open a large spiked fruit
and scoops the arils out of the hull,
hands them to you on red plastic plates.
You sit on a crumbling concrete landing
and suck the pungent flesh
off thick flat seeds
until you both are thoroughly satisfied.

To find your way back
you retrace your steps
by landmarks you remember passing:
a pharmacy window,
an empty beer hall,
a banyan tree next to a streetlamp.
You stop at each crossroads
to make sure you agree
that you're headed in the right direction.

This is how it is with a new lover, you think:
hunger awake, watching for signs,
finding your way
along a foreign path
that you've traveled on before.

II. Sketches of India

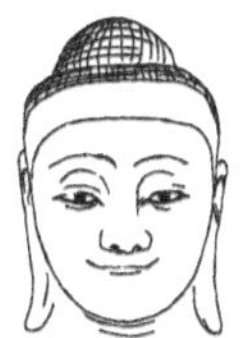

Tiruvannamalai

A group of boys gather in a dirt clearing,
picking sides for a game of cricket.

An old man squats against a tree stump,
smokes a cigarette,
watching.

In the distance, Arunachala,
the great mountain,
is silent.

Three cows graze and flop their tails
in the high grass.

On the Way to Yogi Ramsuratkumar Ashram for Chanting

Before dawn random people mill about,
apparitions in the darkness.
Pujas have begun in the temples.
The air is fresh with cow dung.
You walk along a dirt road
on your way to chanting.
A man leans against the side of a building,
smoking, you know by the orange glow
of his beedi, his body eclipsed in shadow.
Up ahead three young women in red saris
walk side by side without speaking,
their skin deep brown, Dravidian.
For a moment you think of going
wherever they are going.
In the distance: bells, singing.

The Godchild of Tiruvannamalai

Flashback, 1991

As they sat side by side on the outskirts of Tiruvannamalai, on a patio shaded from the Indian sun, in a field of wild grass dotted by trees, Yogi Ramsuratkumar, who referred to himself as *this dirty beggar,* and really was dirty, and a real-life beggar, turned to his disciple, a formidable master himself, and fingered the stud in his earlobe. "Is it a real diamond?" he asked. "No," Lee said. "It's not real?" the yogi said, wide-eyed, playful. "It's made of glass," said the younger master. The dirty beggar slapped Lee's leg and laughed. "The fake diamond glitters more than the real," he said. He slapped Lee's leg and laughed. "The fake diamond glitters more than the real!"

Temple Commerce

Arunachalesvara Temple, Tiruvannamalai

You leave your shoes with a group
of boys who for two rupees will make sure
that nobody steals them.
They are numbered and added
to neat rows of sandals and flip-flops—
valet parking for the pedestrian seeker.
The entrance hall is blocked by a mob of beggars—
some old, some women, some children.
They make hand-to-mouth gestures,
tug upon your sleeves. They will eat you alive
if you don't push your way through them.

Inside, the temple priest (thank God!)
is not averse to taking bribes.
You are ushered down a stone corridor,
down a spiraling series of ancient steps,
to the inner sanctum
where a stone lingam emanates heat
from the core of the earth.
You get a red smudge on your forehead
and a postcard for prasad.
The lingam makes you sweat.

In the courtyard
a sadhu dressed like Shiva
wears faux tiger skin pants.
He wants to bless you
for a small donation.
You count your blessings
as he counts your cash.

Anandashram

Your first morning on Anandashram
you are eager to dress
and walk to the bhajan hall.
Twenty years ago,
as a very young man,
you played an all-day game of cards here
with your American master
during a visit to pay homage to his lineage.
Concession is the better part of valor, he'd said,
laughing, when you overbid your partner
to disastrous results.
You were embarrassed to not know
the meaning of the word *concession*.
He patiently explained,
without making you feel small.
His bony nose and perfect grin,
the way he looked you in the eye,
is etched like a jewel in your memory.

5 a.m. is the Vishnu Sahasranamam,
chanted in Sanskrit.
You don't know the words
so you close your eyes and listen.
5:30 is Rambhajan, call and response,
slowly, *Om Shri Ram Jai Ram Jai Jai Ram*,
drawn out to the pace of a harmonium.
At 6 a.m. sadhus in orange line up
for coffee and chai.
You file in among them
to the open-air cafeteria,

find a quiet place in the corner
with your notebook.
A man in white Indian pajamas and a Muslim topi
comes by to refill your cup
from a dented tin teapot.
Please, he says, as he serves you.
You lower your head to thank him.

Then the sun.
The glorious sun.
Shining light on Kerala.

Two Jungles

Kerala

Bhagawan Nityananda was a large man with a massive belly and a great bald head, considered by many to be the highest of realized beings. He wandered India in nothing but a loincloth and sometimes didn't bother to wear that. He walked into a jungle in Kerala, found a deep and narrow cave, sat down in the back of it where the ceiling and walls barely fit his massive frame. He sat in samadhi for days, weeks, months at a time, among scorpions, bats, and snakes, without eating. If he felt like drinking something he emerged from the cave, smashed open a coconut, went back in. When his disciples finally found him and wished to build a temple on this holy site, Nityananda picked up a stone, threw it hard against the ground, from which spot burst forth a spring of clear water. He told his disciples that this water was the Ganga. They built the temple around it. That's how the story goes.

Half a century later a slightly built priest, an old brown man, offers water, fire, incense, rice all day long to a statue of Nityananda. He tells you that it rains there six months of the year. Temperatures soar past 100 degrees in summer. The jungle is throbbing, teeming with insects, bird calls, humidity and heat. You feel the dark heart of it beating back to ancient times.

When you look into the eyes of the priest
you see two jungles
have changed him.

The Young Man on the Train

from Kerala to Mumbai

The young man on the train has been making noise
since he boarded the 4:30 stop at Goa,
keeps the light on when all around
are trying to sleep, plays music
on his cell phone, walks up and down the aisle
spying women in their bunks.
He's worked hard to cultivate his style:
sideburns, mustache, slicked-back hair,
tight-fit jeans, green button-down shirt—
surely the best his modest rupee can buy.
He talks to anyone who will listen.
He wants to live a good life.
As I study him, I am filled
with sorrow.

Boys on an Ashram

Shanti Mandir Ashram, Gujarat

Boys chanting Sanskrit
on an ashram.

The setting sun gives rise
to vast space.

A boy offers fire
to the Guru.

The Guru is a fire
that consumes the self.

The world beyond these walls
is a dark and dying place.

God is kept alive
by praise.

Haridwar

Very old buildings of varying heights and hues
stacked tightly against each other
like children's blocks
line the west bank of the Ganga.
The Ganga pouring down wide
from the Himalayas
with deceptive force and speed.

You've woken up early
to sit in meditation
with your traveling sangha
in a small room against the river.
Just this and the sound of water
lapping against your shores.

Someone is doing puja on the far shore.
You hear the lone clanging of a bell.

The best thing about being in this body
is five senses connecting you to all things.

Fakir Poet

It is dark when you pass.
At first you don't see him.
A man on a small carpet
sitting against a brick wall
along a narrow side street
of a marketplace.
He sits cross-legged
with a one-string ektara across his lap,
plucks the string with a finger of his right hand,
keeps beat against the gourd body
with bells on the fingers of his left.
He sings with his eyes closed
in a language you don't understand,
though you hear in his voice
a familiar longing.
You are not sure he is aware you are there.
Even when you drop a ten-rupee note
in his begging bowl.
You stand quietly and listen,
not wanting to distract him
from his true audience.
A man against a wall in the dark
singing a song of the heart.

Rain in Haridwar

Some say that rain is auspicious
at the beginning or end of a venture.
Our last day in Haridwar
we wake up to thunder and rain.
It hammers down hard on the Ganga.
She takes it into her body like anything else.
Hotel staff stack our bags on a bicycle rickshaw.
A man in full rain gear straps a tarp over it
and pedals off.
We climb into motorized rickshaws
and zip through the marketplace
toward the train station.
The narrow turns of the market
are flooded with garbage and rain.
A man standing on the steps of a doorway
lights a beedi as small rivers
rush down the slope at his feet.
A chai wallah beneath an awning
stirs a pot of steaming milk.
We are headed to Delhi
from where we will go our separate ways.
India goes on like the sidelong dream
of a slumbering giant.

The Coldest Morning of the Year in Delhi

you wake up before the rest of your group
and go out in search of coffee.
You wander into a slum and buy a cup of chai
from a ramshackle stall beneath a tree.
Twenty feet away six men feed a fire
from a pile of cardboard, sacks, and rags.

This is how it looks when the world begins to burn.

You walk over and stand behind them.
They make room for you to squat beside them.
They are too beat up to speak.
You are strangely glad for the silence.
They warm their hands.
You warm your hands.
Fourteen hands around a fire.

III. Ashes

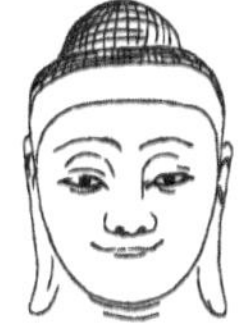

Both

Someday you will both write poetry about this time,
he said, when you were ten years old
and wanted nothing to do with me.
Friday afternoons I picked you up
from school in San Francisco
and drove you back across the bridge
through Berkeley
to your grandmother's house
for the weekend. Those forty-five minutes
in the car the extent of our time together
for that week. Your mother dressed you
in bell-bottom jeans and embroidered shirts
that she'd found in vintage clothing stores,
though her own style was Los Angeles goth.
You had questions.
Where were you living when I was two?
How many times did you see me
when I was four?
You'd already memorized the answers.
You were testing me
to see how honest I could be.

Now you are a short walk away
on this ashram, as is that man
who gave me guidance.
He with a shrine to house his hallowed bones,
where seekers come on pilgrimage.
You beneath an unmarked stupa
on a hillside where ravens nest
in black and wild glory.

Did he really think you would be a poet?

Or did he see one of us
on a splintered bench
with a notebook, the other
ash and memory, continuing
a conversation
that started on a bridge
and is not easily answered.

What She Carried

A father who left her to wolves
in a stark Las Vegas apartment.
A mother who taught her
that all men leave.
A father who came back
years later, wanting to make things right.
A mother who moved her to a faraway city
to spare her confusion.
A love of books
and music on vinyl
in a world going out of style.
Dismay at the ways
humans hurt
each other.
A childhood moving up and down
the West Coast, her closest friends
adults her mother had over on weekends

until her final year of high school
when she found a place
among misfits
and a boyfriend
who showed her

how to quiet
the ache
with a needle to the arm.

When I went up to Oregon
to claim her body from a campsite
the sheriff handed me a backpack
with her belongings inside.

She had a paperback copy
of *As I Lay Dying*, a pack of cigarettes
and a diary, which I could not bear to read.

The Day We Buried You

The day we buried you
your mother was too broken to be there.
Clélia, your stepmother, my ex-wife, was there.
And my dearest friend Nara,
who chose the spot, on a hillside
in front of a very short tree.
I dug a hole a couple of feet deep
and poured your ashes from a plain black urn into it.
We found a flat-faced, rectangular-shaped rock,
a natural perfect headstone,
and placed it in front of the tree.
And then another flat rock,
a half foot thick, about two feet long,
with earth-sculpted bends in it,
that somehow resembled the armless, legless
torso of a child's body.
We lay that most extraordinary rock
on the spot above your ashes, stood back
and marveled at it.
We gathered an assortment of stones
and formed a circle around the whole thing
until each end closed at the headstone.
We spread out then
looking for the shiniest pieces of white quartz
we could find—they were plentiful—
and gradually filled the space within the circle.
As we did so it began to rain,
a fine desert rain
through which shone a translucent light
some would describe as miraculous.

We worked in silence. In the rain.
In the God-given light,
creating something worthy
of your memory.
None of us knew what to say.
I still do not know what to say.
I'm still not saying it.

The Mountain and the Monk

Every morning I sit on this mountain
and watch my thoughts swirl and disappear
into the great river of mind.
I've given up my robes.
I've given up my seat in the temple.
I've given up my name.
None of those things could save me.

I have been a thoughtless man,
banished from the company of others
because for too long I sought my own
pleasure and gain at the expense
of ones who needed me.

Now I sit alone on this mountain,
through wind and sun and snow,
in this second life
and I pray for the seasons
to break me down.

This mountain has gotten inside me.
I hear it rumbling through my hollow bones.
It rises in me like a dark sun, sure
and devastating,
slower than the slowest time,
until I no longer know
if what remains is me
or the mountain.

Li Po walked down from the mountains

in his sandals, with a rucksack and a notebook, and took a counter stool at a truck stop diner. The waitress walked over with a pencil behind her ear and called him *sweetheart* as she poured him a cup of black coffee. Li Po ordered eggs sunny side up, hash browns, and a side of bacon. He looked around and sipped his coffee while he waited for his food. He was hungry after a long night walking through forests.

Truckers in cowboy hats and baseball caps lined the long counter, hunched over newspapers and breakfast plates, some of them smoking cigarettes. Li Po turned to the trucker on his left and said, "Excuse me, sir, I'm looking for a ride to the shores of the Yangtze River." The trucker looked him over and said, "I don't know where that is, partner," then went back to reading the news. Li Po squinted into his coffee mug, cupped between his palms, and looked to the waitress for a refill. Nobody knew who he was or where he was going.

1989 Prescott Arizona

Back in the day
we were on a drunk
and my friend, a literary nerd
from New York City,
asked the questions
as we sat around a fire
under an old railroad bridge
with a couple of Navajo,
who were a long way from home
and also on a drunk,
opening 12-oz cans of beer
and passing cigarettes.

*What do you think is the difference between
a White man and an Indian?* my friend asked,
as I cringed.

You see a town with trees growing in it,
the talkative one said. *We see a forest
with buildings and concrete on top of it.*

I was thinking about the world as a forest,
how the machine beast of modernity
chews up every last thing in its path,
as I crumpled up an empty pack of Camels
and tossed it in the fire.
The talker leaned over and put his hand on my wrist.
We don't burn garbage in our fires, he said.

That made more sense than anything
anyone had said to me in months, probably years.

Though we were all burning garbage
in our fires that night.

Cousins

After dark, in a neighborhood
with no streetlights, where men
peering out from curtained rooms
guard muscle cars with guns,
my cousins and I steal chrome valve caps
off custom wheels and screw them
to the Tuff Wheels of our BMX bikes.

In daylight we ride muddy trails
through Wildcat Canyon,
sit beneath a tree by a creek bed,
smoke cigarettes lifted
from my uncle's cartons,
trade stories of wild dogs
that roam the hills in packs
attacking at random.

The stories have been passed down
from older kids to the young
as far back as anyone can remember.
We know they aren't true.
We tell them anyway.

It's early November, 1979.
We are not yet old enough to drive.
Once we are, we'll find real trouble.

Elegy for the Oakland Raiders

It was the end of boyhood
when the Oakland Raiders
packed up their shoulder pads
and their swashbuckling renegade heroes
and drove a long truck down the road
to Los Angeles in the dead of night.
Like any first-time jilted lover,
I watched from afar, mistaking
their victories for my own,
mourning defeat, holding out hope
that one day they would come to their senses
and return to their rightful place beside me.
And they did return, after fourteen years
of neglect, to the land of their birth,
to the fanbase that adored them.
Though as happens when a lover
has stayed too long in the arms of another,
the team that came home was nothing like
the one I remembered going.

No One Here Gets Out Alive

I must have been sixteen
when I took down the posters
above my bed
of Cheryl Ladd and Jaclyn Smith
in beach bikinis
with contoured stomachs
and lipstick smiles
– Charlie's sexiest angels –
and replaced them
with a leather-collared close-up
of Jim Morrison.

When my father ripped Morrison off the wall
I returned the next day
to Hilltop Mall
and bought a replacement.
A shouting match ensued.
Me standing guard at the poster.
My mother in the middle.
My father rage-faced,
thrusting a pointed finger at Morrison,
then at me, making threats
that he would never follow through on.

It felt pointless to even try to explain
that I had just read *No One Here Gets Out Alive*
and everything had changed.
That I was on a new diet
of psilocybin mushrooms
and cannabis sativa

and my mind had become a fledgling sun
rising up behind a mountain,
seeing the world for the first time.

My father was a high-school basketball legend
from a coal-mining town
who turned down a college scholarship
to move to California and raise a family.
He busted his ass at blue-collar jobs.
He was a good man.

His boy was no All-American.

Washed by Time

I.
Paul Madigan was the son of a doctor
and a dead ringer for Tom Petty.
He cultivated the look,
grew his blonde hair out,
wore clothes that Petty might wear
onstage.

What was I to say?
In my black leather jacket,
lugging around books
by William Blake and Frederich Nietzsche,
writing poems that mimicked
Jim Morrison.

It was 1983. We were seniors
at an all-boys Catholic school
where the Salesian Brotherhood
had eyes for teenage ass.

II.
It was the backseat of a chartered bus
on the last day of school
on the way back from a field trip
to an amusement park
where Paul told me the story,
a confession really, of an older relative
who slipped something in Paul's beer
at a family gathering
and later had his way with him,

Paul as good as paralyzed
behind a closed door.
He was sore the next day,
but remembered
through the drug-induced haze
that his dick stayed hard the whole time.
Does that mean that I liked it? he said.
I didn't know what to say.
You shouldn't have let him do that, I said.
That was the last time we spoke
to each other.

III.
We had some good times,
driving the bridge to San Francisco
on a Saturday night,
Paul singing along to American Girl
in the brand new 280Z
that his father bought for him.
We drank beers in the alley
behind The Lusty Lady
before sneaking past the doorman
to the peep show.
When we ran out of quarters
we used fingernail clippers
to cut through the chickenwire
above our booth
and climbed onto the ceiling
where we hoped to view the dance floor
for free. I fell through first,
landing on my feet in a hallway
and then Paul crashed down

among the dancers
and was swarmed by a mob
of real live nude girls
with real-life tits
and pubic hair
and beaten with the spiked ends
of high-heeled shoes
until the doorman raced in
to finish him.
Somehow Paul got out
through the fire escape
and jumped from the bottom rung of the ladder
into the alley, where we hid in the shadows
then ran for the Z as a firetruck
and small army of police cars
arrived on the scene.

IV.
Though he did alright
with the public school girls,
who seemed drawn to his aura
of stardom, it was hard for me to respect
Paul's alter-ego obsession.
I thought Petty too much the pop star.
I liked The Doors, of course,
60s psychedelia, and guitar bands
with dark chord progressions.

But some things are washed by time
and in my later days, I've developed
a peculiar affection for the music
of Tom Petty.

V.
Paul, if you could see
the hipsters smirk
when I go on about

his underrated songwriting
and understated style.

They don't know how it feels.

They don't know how it feels.

They don't know how it feels
to be me…

Ghost Town

On a Greyhound bus from the East Coast to the West Coast. Late at night. Somewhere on the open plains. We pull into a ghost town for a pitstop. I walk into a dance hall. Through a room of dust-covered tables and chairs. Past an old-time hardwood bar with shelves of half-filled bottles behind it. Find a bathroom in the back. A large open room. Stand at a row of urinals to piss. Zipping up, I feel a presence behind me. Turn to see my 16-year-old self standing and staring. It's me. Brown hair down to my shoulders, in the varsity letterman's jacket that my father insisted on buying, that I posed in for a photograph with my mom, then hung in the back of a closet. "What are you doing here?" I say. My 16-year-old self does not answer. I say it again. "What are you doing here?" I want to know if he has come to deliver a message. Then he is gone. I walk out to the bus. Take my seat by the window. The other passengers have not returned. I look out at the star-filled sky. Watch a stream of headlights appear as the bus, now empty, merges onto the highway.

I heard the news

two years after the fact
when I came across
an outlaw poetry website
that features his work.
It saddened me
not because a man had died
but because there have never been many
like him to begin with.
I talked to him once on the phone
when I was tracking a dishonest editor
from Albuquerque
who had stolen a manuscript.
He had a good laugh at that.
A couple of years later
when I was running a small press magazine
I solicited work from him
and was thrilled with what he sent.
He wrote poems about Dillinger
and other gangsters, blues men,
freight train hustlers,
life beneath the bridge.

i liked him
for his
short
chopped
up lines
that flowed
down the
page with

no capital
ization
or punc
tuation
when you
write it like
that there
is nothing
to hide
behind you
either hit
the mark
or not
Todd Moore
hit it often
enough
sometimes
he blew it
apart

Patron of the Art

I take no pleasure in saying it
because he was generous with me and others
but he was not the best of poets,
though he loved the art
and knew good writing.
When he was not driving a taxi
through the night-soaked streets of Rhode Island
he spent too much time with a bottle
and it made his words fall flat and sloppy.
Not even the whores
with whom he traded services
and were the subjects of his liveliest pieces
could save him.
He wrote it raw. He had the right idea.
Yet there were things I sensed
he wanted to say
that never came through.
He liked to put out broadsides
for poets he thought were up and coming.
That's how I got to know him, briefly,
when he came across my poems
in a small press journal.
I heard he died behind the wheel of his taxi
waiting on a light to turn green.
How lucky is that?
To have one's death write itself.
His notebook on the seat beside him.

Li Po took a driving test

and all he saw was the moon. The examiner said, *Turn left at this intersection.* Li Po waited for the right of way, looked up at the midday sky and saw the faint outline of a moon. The examiner said, *Now parallel park.* As Li Po backed into a spot between two cars, he looked into the rearview mirror and saw a plump-faced moon looking back at him. That night, a brand-new driver's license tucked into his wallet, Li Po took a bottle of rice wine and drove out of the city to celebrate. He drove far out on a lonely country road, where the sky was darker than dark can be, and when a great, drunk, glorious moon rose up from behind a mountain, bathing the world in its glow, Li Po drove straight into it, the bottle of rice wine in his right hand, the other hand reaching out the window, dying to touch the moon.

Genízaro

When I show him the DNA test
he argues with the results, my father
who grew up collecting arrowheads
along the Purgatoire River, hiding them
in shoeboxes beneath his bed, not knowing
it was his own bone and blood
who left them there. Ancestors crowded
into blind arroyos, bound with rope like wild
horses and sold to Spanish bidders. Girls
put to work in fields, in kitchens,
at the call of rough appetites. Boys
raised as soldiers, taught to rain fire
against their own severed memories.

My father sits in his armchair
in front of his flatscreen television
and watches Ancient Aliens, his new obsession,
leaning forward to take in aerial views
of a lost Mayan city overgrown
by jungle. His wife of sixty years,
childlike with dementia,
in her own chair beside him.

During a commercial break
he walks to the kitchen table,
puts his reading glasses on
and runs his fingers
over the chart I've printed out for him.
My father always said we were Spanish, he says.

So many Genízaros who believe they are Spanish.

His Whole Life

My father, who is 82 years old,
who turned down scholarships
because he thought
he wasn't smart enough
for college, tells stories
every chance he gets
about high school basketball
when he was the point guard
on a team of coal miners' sons
who took down giants
from the big city.
He even talks about
his middle-school team
who went 32-0
over the span of two seasons.

Family and friends nod patiently
as if to say, Yes, Abe, you were great,
and that was a long time ago.

What can one say to a man
who is still running down a court
after stealing a pass
en route to an airborne layup,
his whole life rushing up behind him.

Departures

At an unnamed airport, scanning the board for a departing flight, we couldn't find her anywhere, my mother. Until she came running through the terminal in her pink pajamas, white hair flaming, and I ran after her, out a set of double-wide doors, onto a rickety wooden pier in a hidden alcove of a bay. It was dark. She stood at the edge overlooking the water, then turned and looked back as I approached. She knew who I was. Then she spun and dove in with surprising agility.

She swam frog-like, just below the surface, arms and legs jutting out in awkward unison, and rounded the corner of the pier, ten feet out where the waters got rough and deep. My father ran up and I thought I would have to stop him from diving in after her. But he stood beside me and watched as she swam straight down, disappearing from our lives, smoothed over by the current.

The King's Secret

You say it is not you.
But I've seen your hand
outstretched to touch the dying.
They come to you for miracle, salvation,
slow death dragging on them
like sacks of rock slung over the shoulders.
I've seen you in your night robes
with lantern
standing in the royal doorway
to greet them.
They bring you bad dreams, sad lies,
half-hearts half emptied,
clinging to bone-stark hope.
And you don't tell them
it is not within your power
to calm the black winds
blowing curses through their homeland.
You don't tell them
they must accept loss
as you have, forever,
as the great sea opens up
and takes rain like aloneness into its waters.
Whose heart are you shielding?

You say it is not you.
But I've seen you kiss
the open sores of the afflicted.
You think no one is watching
when you take them
into your palace
and clothe them in your garments.

I Find Him in the Dreamworld

I find him in the dreamworld,
as I've found him before,
the man who taught me to fly fish.

That old grizzled man
with tobacco eyes
and a thoughtful gait
who walked a young boy
down a steep ravine
to an ancient shore
of mountain boulders.
Who taught him
to read the mysteries
of rough water, the pull
of long currents, the undercuts
of banks where skittish trout hid
hungry and holding.
Who taught him to balance
a line in his left
with a rod in his right
and drop a feathered fly
softly, precisely where the want
was waiting.
*Make three perfect casts
and move*, he'd say.
*Always keep moving
and fishing upstream.*
The rest the boy figured out on his own.
How to quiet his mind
and be alone on the earth.

That dusk is the hour
to float a mosquito.

I find him in a root cellar,
the outside door ajar,
sitting on a bench
behind a corner table.
He's wearing green coveralls
and his janitor's hat, an old miner's
lunch pail open beside him.
He looks the same age
as the year a white dove
nested in his yard, the year
his heart stopped beating.
I thought you were dead, I say.
We sit in secret exile.
I ask him how it's possible
that he goes on living.

How I've longed to tell him
of the miles upon miles
of wilderness I've wandered
in search of pristine
rivers and streams,
spit-roasting brookies
and browns, cutthroats
and rainbows
for breakfast, lunch, and dinner.
I wish I could have known him as a man,
to sit with him beside a fire,
to drink from ice-cold springs
together.

I knew him as a boy.
He put a long lightweight rod in my hands
and delivered my heart to water.

When the Music's Over

After spending a night in Los Angeles
I drove up Sunset Boulevard
past the Whiskey a Go Go.
Jim Morrison, in his lizard skin,
with his mescaline grin,
was not in there.
I parked in front of a coffee house
run by a young Korean couple.
He in Nike baseball cap.
Her hair dyed pink.
I'd heard they make good coffee.
Six young men sat at separate tables,
headphones on, attention consumed
by laptop screens.
I ordered the East Timor beans
and sat by the corner window,
listened to a muted jazz trumpet.
Across the street in a strip mall:
Angelina's Donuts, Thai Friendly Massage,
a liquor store with windows caged.
A Latino boy walked in from the 80s
wearing a black leather vest,
no shirt underneath,
a scorpion tattooed to his bicep.
The sky was a perfect morning blue.
I walked three blocks
down to Stories bookstore,
browsed the poetry shelf,
picked out a stack to my liking.
Poetry comes through the cracks in this world.
Even as the light dies.

On the Way to Morning Meditation

To walk in the dark I trust
my body. Leave the mind out of it.
How many times my feet have found
every rise and turn of this path
in winter. I let them lead the way.

This morning, a rare low cover
of clouds envelops the high desert.
Faint white shadows shifting places
in the dark. A thick misty rain
caresses my face like the cool
awakening hand of a lover.

It's more than the eye that knows
beauty. The soft wet crunch
of my steps is the music I need.

These Things

after Ryokan

Stepping onto my porch in the morning dark of winter
I smell smoke from my wood stove—
juniper and pine.
An all-night moon sets round on the horizon
casting light on mountain ranges
capped with yesterday's snow.
Something about snow
in the arid high desert
says *beauty is eternal,*
says *everything melts.*
I walk a winding path
to the hall for meditation
and take a front-row seat
in a theater of silence.
A friend tells me of Indian yogis
who stop thought by fixing the mind
on a single spot between the eyebrows—
they say only then does meditation begin.
I'm too lazy to stop my thoughts.
I let them settle and find a course.
They come and go like snow.

Pujari

In my twenties I clawed my way
out of bed to be on time
to the hall for meditation.
Now, in my late fifties,
I wake up early.

I start a fire in the wood stove,
put on water for coffee,
sit at my desk and contemplate lines
that want to say more.

At a quarter to seven, I step out into winter.
This three-minute walk
through darkness, as the earth awakens,
my favorite part of the day.

When the master was alive
people drove in from town
to sit in his presence.

That was a long time ago.
He did not leave a successor.

I light candles around the dais,
burn incense, get the ghee lamp ready
for the waving of lights.
I ring a bell to start time
for two or three elders who straggle in
and take their seats by force of habit.

Will You Miss Me

Before I went on retreat
you packed my bags for me.
A couple of short-sleeve shirts
and long-sleeve Heattechs,
a cashmere sweater for the cold mornings,
two pairs of meditation pants—one thick, one thin—
an Aeropress coffee maker, beans, and a grinder,
various-sized notebooks, and pens,
the essential toiletries.
As I stepped out the door
you said, playfully, "Will you miss me?"
And I said, "I don't know. Maybe.
I've got a lot of work to do up there."
And here I am, on day five,
in this awesome silence, the morning after
a rainy, snowy day in April.
I've already written the pieces I set out to write.
I've gotten clear about the manuscript
I've been fretting over, and made some crucial edits.
I've written that one poem
that I knew I needed to write
but had started to doubt was in me.
And from the window of this hut
I can see, down the canyon,
the chocolate-brown cottage we built together.
I imagine you sitting at your desk,
with your own view up canyon of this retreat center,
working on your own poems,
taking such diligent care to get the words right.
How I adore your peculiar perfectionism.

I do miss you, I confess.
There are moments I ache to see you.
To see you from across the room,
sitting at the kitchen table, composing
one of your sprawling, multifaceted to-do lists.
I've been trying to find ways
to tell you how glad I am
to have you here with me,
not just on this ashram,
but in this life together.
Love seems too trite a word
to describe the feeling that consumed my thoughts
all day yesterday, and nearly drove me to despair.
That I never want to die.
That I never want to leave this world
now that I've found you in it.

The Shade of Your Tree

There are flowers growing next to your gravesite.
A tiny, delicate cluster, reddish-orange,
growing up out of hard, rocky soil.
And a very small tree, no more than
three feet tall, sits right above you,
its black-brown trunk and branches
artfully gnarled like the trees
in the Chinese landscape painting
that hung in the room that you slept in.
I bring it water each time I visit.

But the best thing, the part you would love,
is the patch of soft earth between the
tree and the flat smooth rock that serves
as your headstone. That little patch of earth
is the perfect size for a small desert animal,
perhaps a rabbit, to make its bed.
I imagine it happening, and I smile.
A furry brown cottontail, curling up
under the shade of your tree,
finding refuge from the hot summer sun.

Visiting a Friend

My friend lives up the canyon
at the head of a dry creek bed.
From my porch I see
the slanted roof of his house
nestled beneath a sandstone cliff.
I look to it often.
Between us, the ashram burial grounds
where my daughter's ashes are buried.
When I walk up the canyon to visit my friend
I stop to tend the stones
around her grave.
My friend makes chai and talks about
his meditation practice.
I listen with great interest,
though I am reluctant to talk about my own.
Because there is only so much
one can say about sitting,
soon we are gossiping about the others,
like two old ladies at tea time.

Last night, monsoon rains
danced across the rooftops
in sheets. A blessing in the high desert.
When I walk back down the canyon

I stop again at her grave.
Before a storm took him
Jack Kerouac said, *Accept loss forever.*
The master who was here
said, *Friendship is the way.*

Ashes

after Kobayashi Issa

My daughter's ashes
are buried on a hillside
in the high desert.
I sit on a bench
beneath a pine tree
looking up at her grave.

      This end
of the burial grounds
is the quietest place
on this ashram.
Our lives are but a dewdrop.
This great silence remains.

Notes

"Ode to a British Monk": Suan Mokkh International Dhamma Hermitage was founded by Buddhadasa Bhikkhu (1906-1993). The practice of Anapanasiti taught at Suan Mokhh features what Buddhadasa called "the long breath."

"Ikkyu walked into a ladyboy bar": "Kathoey" is the Thai word traditionally used for transgendered women. "Ladyboy" is the English version of the word and was created by the kathoey community itself to identify themselves to Westerners. Neither term is considered derogatory in Thai culture.

"In a Silent Way": The Kallang River is the longest river in Singapore, flowing for 10 kilometers from the Lower Peirce Reservoir to the Kallang Basin.

The poems in the section "Sketches of India" were written in January 2014 while on pilgrimage with a few members of my sangha. I wrote a poem a day during that 26-day trip and in 2021, when I began writing again in earnest, set about revising them. The twelve poems in this section are what survived that process.

"Anandashram": Swami Ramdas, the founder of Anandashram, was known for his inclusive attitude toward all religions. It is common to see Hindus and Muslims worshipping side by side at Anandashram. This phenomenon is reflected in the line "A man in white Indian pajamas and a Muslim topi."

"Two Jungles": The Nityananda in this poem is Swami Nityananda (late 19th century-1961), who is believed to have been born in Kerala, India and whose ashram is in Ganeshpuri.

"No One Here Gets Out Alive" borrows its title from a bestselling biography of Jim Morrison, written by Jerry Hopkins and Danny

Sugerman (Warner Books, 1980). The book itself takes its title from a line from the Doors song "Five to One," on the album *Waiting for the Sun* (1968).

"Genízaro": Genízaro is the term given to Indigenous populations who were enslaved and detribalized by the Spanish during the colonization of New Mexico (and parts of southern Colorado). When the New Mexico territory was eventually annexed by the United States, many Genízaros, now free, told American settlers and government officials that they were Spanish, thinking it would win them higher status. So many of them told their own children they were Spanish that it is common today for descendants of Genízaros to genuinely believe they are Spanish. For an in-depth study of the history, see *Nación Genízara: Ethnogenesis, Place, and Identity in New Mexico*, edited by Moises Gonzales and Enrique R. Lamadrid (University of New Mexico Press, 2019).

"When the Music's Over": The Doors got their start as the house band at the Whiskey a Go Go during the summer of 1966, where Jim Morrison was known to improvise song lyrics while tripping on LSD. "When the Music's Over" is the title of a song on The Doors' second album, *Strange Days* (1967).

"Will You Miss Me" is for Dominique Ahkong.

"These Things" is loosely after Ryokan's poem "Too Lazy To Be Ambitious."

"Ashes" is after Kobayashi Issa's most famous haiku, written upon the death of his daughter (see this book's epigraph for the haiku). I've borrowed Issa's dew drop metaphor, which is not exclusively his, but is a common metaphor for impermanence in classical Japanese poetry.

Acknowledgments

Thank you to the editors of the following publications in which these poems originally appeared, sometimes in earlier versions:

Atlanta Review: "Li Po took the overnight train" and "The Shade of Your Tree"

Chicago Quarterly Review: "I Find Him in the Dreamworld"

Chiron Review: "1989 Prescott Arizona," "Elegy for the Oakland Raiders," and "Nana"

Cultural Daily: "The Mountain and the Monk" and "The Young Man on the Train"

Free State Review: "Departures"

Jelly Bucket: "On the Way to Yogi Ramsuratkumar Ashram for Chanting"

The Literary Underground: "No One Here Gets Out Alive"

Louisiana Literature: "The Day We Buried You," "These Things," "Visiting a Friend," and "What She Carried"

Main Street Rag: "When the Music's Over"

Moon City Review: "Cousins"

Montserrat Review: "The King's Secret"

Nerve Cowboy: "I Heard the News"

New York Quarterly: "Yangon"

Outskirts: "Li Po walked down from the mountains" and "Ryokan owns a barbershop"

Pirene's Fountain: "Ashes" and "The Broken Buddha"

San Pedro River Review: "Foot Massage"

Slipstream: "In a Silent Way"

Soundings East: "Both"

Talking River Review: "Genízaro" and "His Whole Life"

Trajectory Journal: "Patron of the Art"

Water~Stone Review: "Li Po took a driving test"

Early drafts of several poems from the section "Sketches of India" first appeared as a group, some with different titles, in *Tawagoto* (a community journal of Hohm Sahaj Mandir).

About the Author

After publishing a few dozen poems and short stories in the late 90s and early aughts, **Johnny Cordova** dropped out of the literary scene for 17 years. He began writing poetry again in 2021, upon returning from ten years in Southeast Asia. Recent work appears in *Chicago Quarterly Review, Chiron Review, Louisiana Literature, Moon City Review, Water~Stone Review,* and elsewhere. He lives at Triveni Ashram in northern Arizona, where he co-edits *Shō Poetry Journal* with his wife, poet Dominique Ahkong.